Speak Easy

From Basic Conversation to Simplified Debate

Katsunori Fujioka
Nobuyuki Yamauchi
Neil Heffernan
Shigeki Kanasaki
Shimpei Hashio

KINSEIDO

Kinseido Publishing Co., Ltd.
3-21 Kanda Jimbo-cho, Chiyoda-ku,
Tokyo 101-0051, Japan

Copyright © 2019 by Katsunori Fujioka
　　　　　　　　　Nobuyuki Yamauchi
　　　　　　　　　Neil Heffernan
　　　　　　　　　Shigeki Kanasaki
　　　　　　　　　Shimpei Hashio

All rights reserved. No part of this publication may be reproduced, stored in a retrieval system, or transmitted, in any form or by any means, electronic, mechanical, photocopying, recording or otherwise, without the prior permission of the publisher.

First published 2019 by Kinseido Publishing Co., Ltd.

Design　　　Nampoosha Co., Ltd.
Illustrations　Hayato Kamoshita

音声ファイル無料ダウンロード

https://www.kinsei-do.co.jp/download/4084

この教科書で DL 00 の表示がある箇所の音声は、上記 URL または QR コードにて無料でダウンロードできます。自習用音声としてご活用ください。

- ▶ PC からのダウンロードをお勧めします。スマートフォンなどでダウンロードされる場合は、ダウンロード前に「解凍アプリ」をインストールしてください。
- ▶ URL は、検索ボックスではなくアドレスバー (URL 表示欄) に入力してください。
- ▶ お使いのネットワーク環境によっては、ダウンロードできない場合があります。

CD 00　左記の表示がある箇所の音声は、教室用 CD (Class Audio CD) に収録されています。

はじめに

　本書は、平易な英語を用いてコミュニケーションを行うためのスキルの向上と積極的な態度の育成を目的として編集されています。高等学校までに習得したフレーズや語彙を十分に活用し、シンプルに考え、シンプルに表現することを重視しています。

　本書のもう1つの特長は、会話・ディスカッション・プレゼンテーション・ディベートが、無理なく自然な流れで学習できるように構成されていることです。特に、ディベートのユニットでは、限られた授業時間の中で、学習者が自信をもって、主体的に発言できるようになるための「シンプル・ディベート（Simplified Debate）」という新しいスタイルを提示しています。

　Unit 1 から Unit 5 では、キャンパスライフで用いられる大学生の日常会話をトピックとして、ペアワークを中心に英語で会話することに慣れることを目的とした発信型の練習を繰り返します。Unit 6 と Unit 7 では、さらに、会話の中で賛成や反対などの意見と、その理由や根拠を述べるディスカッションの練習をします。Unit 8 から Unit 10 は、プレゼンテーションの練習です。写真や時間割、グラフなどを利用しながら、簡潔なプレゼンテーションのモデルを習得し、1分程度の英語プレゼンテーションができるように導きます。Unit 11 から Unit 15 では、英語で行うディベートを取り上げています。ディベート初心者にも実践可能な「シンプル・ディベート」の方法を用い、簡潔な表現や定型表現と簡略化された形式を活用することにより、ディベート形式の学習が授業内でも可能となるように工夫しています。本書を通して、学習者の皆さんが、自信をもって楽しく気軽に、英語で発言できるようになることを願っています。

　最後になりましたが、本書を作成するにあたり、金星堂の佐藤求太様ならびに松本明子様には、企画の段階から校正に至るまで、貴重なご助言をいただきました。この場をお借りして、心からお礼申し上げます。

2019年1月

著者一同

Speak Easy
From Basic Conversation to Simplified Debate

Table of Contents

Conversation

Unit ❶ Conversation 1
初対面の挨拶をしよう ………………………………………………… 2

Unit ❷ Conversation 2
出身地について話そう ………………………………………………… 6

Unit ❸ Conversation 3
普段の習慣とその頻度について話そう ……………………………… 10

Unit ❹ Conversation 4
過去の出来事について話そう ………………………………………… 14

Unit ❺ Conversation 5
未来やこれからの予定について話そう ……………………………… 18

Discussion

Unit ❻ Discussion 1
自分の意見を述べよう ………………………………………………… 22

Unit ❼ Discussion 2
理由と度合いを示して同意・反論しよう …………………………… 26

Presentation

Unit ⑧ Presentation 1
　　プレゼンテーションの基本構造［出だしと結び］ ················ 30

Unit ⑨ Presentation 2
　　プレゼンテーションの具体的な内容［ボディ］ ················ 35

Unit ⑩ Presentation 3
　　グラフを使ったプレゼンテーション ································ 40

Simplified Debate

Unit ⑪ Simplified Debate 1
　　主張の理由や具体例を示す ·· 46

Unit ⑫ Simplified Debate 2
　　理由や具体例を示して立論する ·· 51

Unit ⑬ Simplified Debate 3
　　相手の立論に反論する ·· 56

Unit ⑭ Simplified Debate 4
　　立場や見方を変えて反論を発想する ································ 61

Unit ⑮ Simplified Debate 5
　　聴衆の立場で評価する ·· 66

巻末資料　基本文法 ·· 72

Unit 1

Conversation 1

初対面の挨拶をしよう

Introduction

DL 02　CD 02

Kenta: Hi. I'm Kenta Nagano. I'm a junior in the Faculty of Engineering.
Yumi: Hello. I'm Yumi Yamada. I'm a first-year student in the Faculty of International Studies.
Kenta: Nice to meet you, Yumi.
Yumi: Nice to meet you, too, Kenta.

　初対面の挨拶では、名前に加え、自分の所属をはっきりと伝えることが大切です。大学生の場合は、大学名、学部あるいは学科名、学年が自分の所属情報になります。スピーチやプレゼンテーションを行う場合にも、初めにこの情報をはっきりと伝えることが重要です。

大学生の学年と主な学部名・学科名

学年

1年生：a first-year student　　2年生：a sophomore　　3年生：a junior　　4年生：a senior

学部、学科　〜学部：the Faculty of 〜　　〜学科：the Department of 〜

the Faculty of International Studies　国際学部　　the Department of Economics　経済学科
経済学：economics　　経営学：business administration　　文学：letters
法学：law　　商学：commercial science　　人文学：humanities
国際学：international studies　　工学：engineering　　理学：science
農学：agriculture　　情報科学：information science　　教育学：education
看護学：nursing　　福祉学：welfare　　スポーツ科学：sports science

Warm-up

Exercise 1

日本語に合わせて、空所にふさわしい語を書き入れ、英文を完成させましょう。

1. タクヤは、スポーツ科学部の2年生です。

   Takuya is a _____ in the Faculty of _____ _____.

2. ミカは、経済学部の3年生です。

   Mika is a _____ in the Faculty of _____.

3. ケイコは、京阪大学看護学部福祉学科の4年生です。

   Keiko is a _____ in the Department of _____, in the Faculty of _____ at Keihan University.

4. 私は、_____大学_____学部_____学科の___年生です。

   I am a _____ in the Department of _____, in the Faculty of _____ at _____.

Exercise 2

DL 03　CD 03

クラスメイトとペアになり、以下の会話文の下線部を替え、初対面の友達との挨拶の練習をしましょう。

Mai: Hello. I am <u>Mai Saito</u>. I'm a <u>first-year student</u> in the Faculty of <u>Business Administration</u>.
Taku: Hi, <u>Mai</u>. I am <u>Taku Okada</u>. I'm <u>a junior</u> in the Faculty of <u>Education</u>.
Mai: Nice to meet you, <u>Taku</u>.
Taku: Nice to meet you, too, <u>Mai</u>.

Reading

「コミュニケーション学概論」を担当するChen教授が教室に入って来ました。初めの挨拶を読んで、内容を確認しましょう。　🎧 DL 04　💿 CD 04

　Good morning, everyone. This course is Introduction to Communication Science. I am your instructor, Ray Chen. I am a professor of psychology in the Faculty of Letters. My office is on the seventh floor in Building #9. It's in front of the cafeteria. Before starting today's lecture, I would like you to get to know each other. When you meet a person for the first time, you usually tell them your name and what faculty you belong to. In your case, you should give your name, what year you are in, and your faculty. Why don't you talk to the students sitting next to you? Find out their names, what year they are in, and their faculties. Then, you can become friends. Don't be shy!

NOTES
Communication Science「コミュニケーション学」　instructor「担当教員」
psychology「心理学」　in front of ~「~の前に」　get to know「知り合いになる」
what faculty you belong to「あなたはどの学部に所属しているか」

Important Expressions

本文に出てきた表現を使って、以下の英文を完成させましょう。

1. プレゼンテーションを始める前に、皆さんに子供時代のことを思い出して欲しいです。

　_____ starting my presentation, I would _____ you _____ think about your childhood.

2. 外に出て、休憩してはどうですか。

　_____ _____ you go out and take a break?

3. これらの表現を10回繰り返しましょう。そうすれば簡単に覚えられますよ。

　Repeat these expressions ten times. _____, you _____ memorize them easily.

Conversation

Listen to the Conversation   DL 05   CD 05

KateとShunが大学の構内で初めて会いました。2人の会話を聴き、空所にふさわしい語を書き入れましょう。

Kate: Hello. My name is Kate Miller. I'm a 1._____ _____ in the Faculty of Humanities.

Shun: I'm Shun Tanaka. I'm a 2._____ in the Faculty of Information Science.

Kate: Nice to meet you, Shun.

Shun: Nice to meet you, too, Kate.

Kate: Could you tell me 3._____ Music Hall is?

Shun: It's 4._____ the second floor 5._____ Building #6.

Kate: Where is Building #6?

Shun: It's 6._____ _____ _____ the library. Can you see the large white building over there? That's the library.

Kate: Thank you. See you later, Shun.

Shun: Have a 7._____ _____, Kate.

Let's Practice

会話を完成させたら、初対面の挨拶をする時の表現を意識しながら、ペアになって会話の練習をしましょう。

Unit 2

Conversation 2

出身地について話そう

Introduction

> **Yumi:** Where are you from, Kenta?
> **Kenta:** I'm from Matsuyama City in Ehime.
> **Yumi:** What is Ehime famous for?
> **Kenta:** It's famous for its oranges and hot springs.

　会話を楽しむには、相手に興味を持つことが大切です。
　挨拶の後は、出会った友達とお互いの出身地について話してみましょう。相手の出身地が分かったら、次に、何が有名か尋ねてみましょう。

▸ 出身地を尋ねる

Where are you from?　どちらの出身ですか。
— I'm from Okayama.　岡山です。[岡山出身です。]
Where is your hometown?　故郷はどちらですか。
— My hometown is Tokushima.　私の故郷は徳島です。

▸ 何が有名か尋ねる

What is Okayama **famous for?**　岡山は、何が有名ですか。
— It is famous for its peaches and grapes.　桃やぶどうで有名です。
What is popular in Tokushima?　徳島では、何が人気ですか。
— The Awa dance is popular there.　そこでは、阿波踊りが人気です。

Warm-up

Exercise 1

日本語に合わせて、空所にふさわしい語を書き入れ、英文を完成させましょう。

1. 奈良は、何が有名ですか。

   _____ is Nara famous _____?

2. 奈良は、古いお寺や神社で有名です。

   Nara _____ _____ _____ its old temples and shrines.

3. 香川では、何が人気がありますか。

   _____ is _____ in Kagawa?

4. そこでは、うどんと栗林公園が人気があります。

   Udon noodles _____ Ritsurin-koen Park _____ popular there.

Exercise 2

🎧 DL 07　💿 CD 07

クラスメイトとペアになり、以下の会話文の下線部を替え、出身地について話す練習をしましょう。

Mai: Where are you from, Taku?
Taku: I'm from Yamagata.
Mai: What is Yamagata famous for?
Taku: It's famous for its cherries and beef.

Unit 2　Conversation 2

Reading

Kentaが自分の出身地を紹介しています。何が有名なのでしょうか。英文を読んで、確認しましょう。

DL 08　CD 08

　　Hello. I'm Kenta Nagano. I'm from Matsuyama City in Ehime. Ehime is famous for its oranges and hot springs. Dogo Hot Spring is one of the oldest hot springs in Japan. There is a beautiful castle in the city. Its name is Matsuyama Castle. It is popular among tourists. It is located on the top of the hill in the center of the city. It is nice to look around the city from the top floor of the castle. Ehime is also famous for its towels. Towels are produced in Imabari City. The brand name Imabari Towel is now popular all over Japan. When you come to Ehime, you should take a hot spring bath, wipe your body with an Imabari Towel, and drink freshly squeezed orange juice.

NOTES
　be located「位置する」　be produced in ~「~産の、~で生産された」
　freshly squeezed「新鮮な搾りたての」

Important Expressions

本文に出てきた表現を使って、以下の英文を完成させましょう。

1. 金沢の兼六園は、日本の三大名園の一つです。

   Kenrokuen Park in Kanazawa is _____ _____ _____ three most famous gardens in Japan.

2. 日本のピアノは、すべて静岡県浜松市で生産されています。

   All the pianos in Japan _____ _____ in Hamamatsu City, Shizuoka Prefecture.

3. 姫路に来る時は、姫路城を訪問するべきです。

   _____ you _____ to Himeji, you _____ visit Himeji Castle.

Conversation

Listen to the Conversation

KateがShunに出身地について尋ねています。2人の会話を聴き、空所にふさわしい語を書き入れましょう。

Kate: Where 1._____ _____ from, Shun?
Shun: I'm from Yamanashi.
Kate: 2._____ is Yamanashi famous for?
Shun: It's famous for its 3._____ and 4._____.
Kate: What do you like about your hometown?
Shun: It is surrounded by mountains, 5._____ it is rich in nature.
Kate: What do you enjoy 6._____ in your hometown?
Shun: I enjoy mountain climbing and 7._____. In 8._____, I enjoy snowboarding with my friends.
Kate: It seems like there is lots to do. I'd love to 9._____ your hometown someday.

NOTES
be surrounded by ~「~に囲まれている」 rich in nature「自然が豊かな」
mountain climbing「登山」 snowboarding「スノーボード」 seem like ~「~のように見える」

Let's Practice

会話を完成させたら、出身地について話す表現を意識しながら、ペアになって会話の練習をしましょう。

Unit 3

Conversation 3

普段の習慣とその頻度について話そう

Introduction

🎧 DL 10 💿 CD 10

Yumi: What time do you get up every morning?
Kenta: I usually get up at 8 o'clock.
Yumi: Do you eat breakfast?
Kenta: No, I seldom do. Instead, I often eat brunch.

　日常生活の習慣について話す時に、その頻度についての情報が加わると、より内容が深まります。習慣的な行為と共に用いられる表現に、頻度の副詞（always, usually, often, sometimes, seldom, never）があります。ここでは、100%の頻度で起こる（絶対確実に起こる）ことを表すalwaysから、0%の頻度で起こりうる（絶対確実に起こらない）ことを表すneverまで、頻度の副詞の尺度を確認し、さらに具体的な回数を述べる表現も確認しましょう。

頻度の副詞

100%	always	「常に」「必ず」
80%	usually	「普通は」
60%	often	「よく」「しばしば」
50%	sometimes	「時々」
20%	seldom, rarely	「めったに〜ない」「ほとんど〜ない」
0%	never	「決して〜ない」「全く〜ない」「一度も〜ない」

具体的な回数を述べる場合 [日／週／月／年に〜回]

once a week「週に1回」　**twice** a month「月に2回」　**three times** a year「年に3回」
I text my friends **five times** a day.　私は、友だちに一日に5回メールします。

Warm-up

Exercise 1

日本語に合わせて、空所にふさわしい語を書き入れ、英文を完成させましょう。

1. 私は、普通は［＝80％の頻度で］バスで登校します。

   I _____ go to school by bus.

2. 父は、常に［＝100％の頻度で］朝食を食べます。

   My father _____ eats breakfast.

3. カナは、めったに［＝20％の頻度で］授業に遅刻しません。

   Kana is _____ late for classes.

4. マリエは、時々［＝50％の頻度で］友人とショッピングを楽しみます。

   Marie _____ enjoys shopping with her friends.

Exercise 2

DL 11　CD 11

クラスメイトとペアになり、以下の会話文の下線部を替え、放課後の活動について話す練習をしましょう。

Taku: What do you usually do after school?
Mai: I usually practice judo.
Taku: How often do you practice judo?
Mai: I practice judo six times a week.

Unit 3　Conversation 3

Reading

身体を動かすことが大好きなKeikoの一日の様子です。Keikoの夢は何でしょうか。英文を読んで、確認しましょう。

DL 12　CD 12

Keiko is a sophomore in the Faculty of Sports Science at Keihan University in Osaka. She likes exercising. She usually jogs for an hour in the morning. At university she studies hard because she wants to get her elementary school teacher's license. She is interested in education and sports theory. She goes to a swimming pool near her house five times a week. She always swims for two hours. She plans to participate in two swimming competitions this year. She sometimes does yoga after swimming for relaxation. Her dream is to become an elementary school teacher and teach children how to swim.

NOTES
exercising「体を動かすこと」　teacher's license「教員免許状」　theory「理論」
participate in ~「〜に参加する」　competition「競技会」

Important Expressions

本文に出てきた表現を使って、以下の英文を完成させましょう。

1. ユミは、たいてい夜に２時間英語を勉強します。

   Yumi usually studies English _____ _____ _____ in the evening.

2. ケンタとシュンは、週４回サッカーをします。

   Kenta and Shun play soccer _____ _____ _____ week.

3. 母は料理が好きで、私によく料理の仕方を教えてくれます。

   My mother likes _____ and often teaches me _____ _____ _____ .

Conversation

Listen to the Conversation

🎧 DL 13 💿 CD 13

MikiがPaulの普段の生活について尋ねています。2人の会話を聴き、空所にふさわしい語を書き入れましょう。

Miki: How ¹._____ times a week do you eat out?
Paul: I ²._____ do. I usually cook for ³._____.
Miki: ⁴._____ do you usually buy groceries?
Paul: I always go to the grocery shop ⁵._____ the station. The vegetables and meat are ⁶._____ and inexpensive.
Miki: How ⁷._____ do you go shopping there?
Paul: I go shopping ⁸._____ a week.
Miki: I hear you work part-time at that grocery shop. ⁹._____ do you work?
Paul: I work ¹⁰._____ _____ on Tuesdays and Fridays.
Miki: How long are your shifts?
Paul: My shifts are usually ¹¹._____ hours.

NOTES
eat out「外食する」 cook for myself「自炊する」 grocery「食料品」 inexpensive「安い」 shift「(アルバイトの) シフト」

Let's Practice

会話を完成させたら、日常生活の習慣についての表現を意識しながら、ペアになって会話の練習をしましょう。

Unit 4

Conversation 4

過去の出来事について
話そう

Introduction

Kenta: What did you do yesterday?
Yumi: I went to a department store near Osaka station.
Kenta: Did you buy anything?
Yumi: Yes, I bought a pair of shoes.

　過去の出来事について話す時には、動詞の過去形を用います。一般動詞の過去形には、規則変化と不規則変化をするものがあります。不規則変化をする動詞には注意しましょう。また、「過去の時間」を示すことにより、いつの出来事であるのかが明確に伝わります。

現在　I **go** to the gym every day.　　私は、毎日ジムに行く。

過去　I **went** to the gym yesterday.　　私は、昨日ジムに行った。[不規則変化の動詞]

▶ 一般動詞の過去形と過去の時間

We **visited** Horyuji Temple last Sunday.　私たちは、先週の日曜に法隆寺を訪れた。
She **volunteered** at a nursing home yesterday.
　　　　　　　　　　　　　　　　　　　　彼女は、昨日介護施設でボランティアをした。
Kenta **got up** at eight fifty this morning.　ケンタは、今朝8時50分に起床した。
They **left** school an hour ago.　彼らは、1時間前に学校を出た。
Yumi **began** to play the piano when she was five years old.
　　　　　　　　　　　　　　　　　　　ユミは、5歳の時にピアノを弾き始めた。
Did you *go* shopping last weekend?　あなたは、この前の週末に買い物に行きましたか。
I **didn't** *take* a bath last night.　私は、昨晩はお風呂に入りませんでした。

Warm-up

Exercise 1

日本語に合わせて、空所にふさわしい語を書き入れ、英文を完成させましょう。

1. 私たちは、去年沖縄に行きました。

    We _____ _____ Okinawa last _____.

2. リエは、10年前に日本のチェス、つまり将棋を指し始めました。(play *shogi*「将棋を指す」)

    Rie _____ to _____ *shogi*, Japanese chess, ten years _____.

3. 私は、昨日3時間数学を勉強しました。

    I _____ mathematics _____ three hours _____.

4. タケシは、去年の冬、脚を骨折しました。

    Takeshi _____ his leg _____ _____.

Exercise 2

DL 15　CD 15

クラスメイトとペアになり、以下の会話文の下線部を替え、放課後の活動について話す練習をしましょう。

Mai: Where did you go after school yesterday?
Taku: I went to the grocery store.
Mai: What did you do there?
Taku: I bought milk, eggs and bananas.

Reading

Yumiは先週の日曜日に友達と遊びました。どこに行って、何をしたのでしょうか。英文を読んで、確認しましょう。

🎧 DL 16 💿 CD 16

I had fun with Tomomi in Wakayama last Sunday. First, we went to an aquarium. We saw many kinds of fish. I liked the sunfish, called *manbo* in Japanese, the best. Tomomi liked the sea turtles. Next, we watched a dolphin show. It was exciting. Then, we went to a souvenir shop. I bought a picture book of dolphins. The pictures of dolphins in the sea are so beautiful. Tomomi found a stuffed sea turtle. I thought it was cute, but Tomomi didn't buy it. She said it was too childish for her. Finally, we ate *ramen* noodles in front of the aquarium. They tasted delicious. It was a fun day.

NOTES

aquarium「水族館」　sunfish「マンボウ」　sea turtle「ウミガメ」　dolphin「イルカ」
souvenir「おみやげ」　picture book「図鑑」　stuffed「ぬいぐるみの」　taste「味がする」
delicious「おいしい」

Important Expressions

本文に出てきた表現を使って、以下の英文を完成させましょう。

1. あなたは、この魚の名前を英語で言えますか。

Can you tell me the name of this fish ＿＿＿＿ ＿＿＿＿?

2. 私は、ペットとして柴犬が一番好きです。

As pets, I like Shiba dogs ＿＿＿＿ ＿＿＿＿.

3. この問題は、私には難しすぎます。

This question is ＿＿＿＿ ＿＿＿＿ for me.

Conversation

Listen to the Conversation

🎧 DL 17   💿 CD 17

KateがShunの高校の時の修学旅行について尋ねています。2人の会話を聴き、空所にふさわしい語を書き入れましょう。

Kate: Where did you go for your high school trip?
Shun: We went to Hokkaido ¹._____ _____. We went skiing there.
Kate: That sounds ²._____. Did you enjoy ³._____?
Shun: Yes, I did. Where did you go, Kate?
Kate: We went to Vancouver, Canada.
Shun: Wow! That sounds ⁴._____! How ⁵._____ _____ you stay there?
Kate: For ⁶._____ three days. I wanted to stay ⁷._____.
Shun: Did you do a homestay?
Kate: No, we ⁸._____. We stayed ⁹._____ _____ hotel. At the moment, I'm planning to join a homestay program in Vancouver for a month.
Shun: Is that why you ¹⁰._____ _____ a part-time job?
Kate: That's ¹¹._____. I want to save money to join the program.

NOTE
save money「お金を貯める」

Let's Practice

会話文を完成させたら、過去形の表現を意識しながら、ペアになって会話の練習をしましょう。

Unit 5

Conversation 5

未来やこれからの
予定について話そう

Introduction

DL 18　CD 18

Yumi: Do you have any plans for summer vacation?
Kenta: Yes. I'm going to go on a trip to England with Paul.
Yumi: What are you going to do in England?
Kenta: We will visit the British Museum in London.

　未来やこれからの予定について話す時には、"be going to" や "will" を用います。"be going to" は「（近いうちに）〜しようと思っている」という話し手の「予定」を表し、"will" は「〜するつもりだ」という話し手の「意志」を表します。また、「未来の時間」を示すことにより、未来やこれからの予定であることがさらに伝わりやすくなります。

　"be going to" や "will" の後には、動詞の原形が来ます。

未来を表す表現と未来の時間

Kenta and Paul **are going to** *visit* London <u>this summer</u>.
　　　　　　　　　　　ケンタとポールは、<u>今年の夏</u>ロンドンに**行く予定だ**。

I'm going to *buy* a birthday present for my mother <u>next Sunday</u>.
　　　　　私は、<u>来週の日曜日に</u>お母さんのために誕生日プレゼントを**買う予定だ**。

I **will** *stay* at home all day <u>tomorrow</u> and *finish* my report.
　　　　　私は、<u>明日</u>は一日中家に居て、レポートを**終わらせるつもりだ**。

We'll *have* a barbecue party <u>this weekend</u>.
　　　　　私たちは、<u>今週末</u>バーベキュー・パーティを**するつもりだ**。

Warm-up

Exercise 1

日本語に合わせて、空所にふさわしい語を書き入れ、英文を完成させましょう。

1. ユキは、今度の日曜日に京都の金閣寺を訪れる予定です。

   Yuki _____ _____ _____ visit Kinkakuji Temple in Kyoto next Sunday.

2. あなたは、今週末に何をする予定ですか。

   What _____ _____ _____ to do this weekend?

3. 私は、明日帰省します。

   I _____ _____ back to my hometown _____.

4. おいしいカレーの作り方を教えてあげましょう。

   I'll _____ you how _____ cook delicious curry.

Exercise 2

クラスメイトとペアになり、以下の会話文の下線部を替え、週末の予定について話す練習をしましょう。

Taku: Where are you going to go this weekend?
Mai: I am going to go to <u>Nagasaki</u>.
Taku: What are you going to do there?
Mai: I will <u>visit Glover Garden and Dejima</u>.

Reading

MikiとYumiが所属するブラスバンド部では、夏にスペシャルコンサートを企画しています。理由は何でしょうか。英文を読んで、確認しましょう。 　DL 20　　CD 20

Miki and Yumi belong to the school brass band. Miki plays the flute and Yumi plays the trumpet. Their band usually gives a concert in April. They invite first-year students to the concert for free. So, they practiced hard during the spring break. This year they are going to give a special summer concert on campus in July. They are going to perform both classical and pop music. They want many students to come to the concert, because they think the more students they have at the concert, the more students will become members of their band.

NOTES
give a concert「コンサートをする」　for free「無料で」　during ~「~の間」　spring break「春休み」
perform「演奏する」

Important Expressions

本文に出てきた表現を使って、以下の英文を完成させましょう。

1. ミキとユミは、バスケットボール部に所属しています。

　　Miki and Yumi ＿＿＿＿＿ ＿＿＿＿＿ the basketball club.

2. 彼女たちは、来週バスケットボールの試合をする予定です。

　　They are ＿＿＿＿＿ ＿＿＿＿＿ have a basketball game ＿＿＿＿＿ week.

3. 夏休みの間、シュンはお金を貯めるために一生懸命働くつもりです。

　　Shun will work ＿＿＿＿＿ to save money ＿＿＿＿＿ the summer break.

Conversation

Listen to the Conversation

🎧 DL 21   💿 CD 21

MikiとPaulがこの夏の予定について話しています。２人の会話を聴き、空所にふさわしい語を書き入れましょう。

Miki: What are you going to do [1]_____ summer vacation?

Paul: I am going to go on a trip to [2]_____ with Kenta.

Miki: Wow! That [3]_____ nice. Which [4]_____ are you going to visit?

Paul: We are going to visit London and Manchester.

Miki: What are you going to do in London?

Paul: We [5]_____ visit Big Ben and the British Museum.

Miki: [6]_____ did you decide to visit Manchester, too?

Paul: Because we [7]_____ _____ and we are big fans of Manchester United. We'd [8]_____ _____ watch a soccer game in Manchester.

Miki: Oh, [9]_____ _____. Have fun in England!

Paul: Thank you. [10]_____ _____ you some [11]_____.

Let's Practice

会話文を完成させたら、未来のことを表す表現を意識しながら、ペアになって会話の練習をしましょう。

Unit 6

Discussion 1

自分の意見を述べよう

Introduction

DL 22　CD 22

> **Yumi:** I think that university students should study English more.
> **Kenta:** Why do you think so?
> **Yumi:** Because it is important for us to communicate in English.
> **Kenta:** I think so, too.

　自分の意見を述べる際には、先に「主張したいこと」をはっきりと述べ、その後に「その理由」を述べます。

主張したいことを述べる

I think that we should use public transportation.　公共交通機関を利用すべきだと思う。
In my opinion, we should not rely too much on the Internet.
　　　　　私の意見では、私たちはインターネットに頼りすぎるべきでない。(rely on ~「~に頼る」)

理由を述べる

... **because** it is convenient and eco-friendly to use public transportation.
　　　　　なぜなら、公共交通機関を利用することは、便利であるし、環境にやさしいからだ。
... **because** information on the Internet is sometimes incorrect.
　　　　　なぜなら、インターネットの情報は時には間違っているからだ。

相手の意見にコメントする

I think so, too. / I don't think so.　私もそう思う。／私はそう思わない。

Warm-up

Exercise 1

日本語に合わせて、空所にふさわしい語を書き入れ、英文を完成させましょう。

1. 人々は、定期的に運動するべきだと思う。
   _____ _____ that people _____ exercise regularly.

2. 私の意見では、父はタバコをやめるべきだ。
   _____ _____ _____ , my father _____ stop smoking.

3. 私たちは、エネルギーを節約することが必要です、なぜなら私たちは、環境を守らなければいけないからです。
   _____ _____ necessary _____ us to save energy _____ we have to protect the environment.

4. 私もそう思います。／私はそう思いません。
   I think _____ , _____ . / I _____ think _____ .

Exercise 2

DL 23 CD 23

クラスメイトとペアになり、以下の会話文の下線部を替え、自分の意見と理由を述べる練習をしましょう。

Taku: I think that we should <u>study Asian languages</u>.
Mai: Why do you think so?
Taku: Because it is <u>important</u> for us to <u>learn about neighboring countries</u>.
Mai: I think so, too. / I don't think so.

NOTE
neighboring「近隣の」

Reading

Kentは街の自動販売機について意見があるようです。どのような意見なのか、英文を読んで、確認しましょう。

DL 24 CD 24

I see vending machines for drinks almost everywhere in our town. In my opinion, we should decrease the number of vending machines. Some people say that it is convenient for us to have them. But do we really need to have them all? I don't think so. I have two reasons for my opinion. The first reason is that they use a lot of electricity. If we decrease the number of them, we will save energy. So, I think this is an eco-friendly option, too. Another reason is that some people buy drinks, drink them on the street, and carelessly throw away empty cans and bottles. So, if we decrease the number of vending machines, we can also decrease littering.

NOTES
vending machine「自動販売機」 decrease「減らす」 the number of ~「~の数」
electricity「電気」 eco-friendly option「環境にやさしい選択」 carelessly「不注意に」
throw away「捨てる」 littering「ゴミのポイ捨て」

Important Expressions

本文に出てきた表現を使って、以下の英文を完成させましょう。

1. タバコの自動販売機の数を減らすべきです。

    We should _____ the _____ of _____ machines for cigarettes.

2. 私たちが英語を勉強することは重要です。

    It is _____ for us _____ _____ English.

3. みんながゴミのポイ捨てをやめれば、町はもっときれいになるでしょう。

    _____ everybody stops _____, our town _____ be cleaner.

Discussion

Listen to the Discussion   DL 25   CD 25

海外留学についての Paul と Miki のディスカッションを聴き、空所にふさわしい語を書き入れましょう。

Paul: Our university offers many study abroad programs.
Miki: I ¹._____ _____ participate in a study abroad program in Australia.
Paul: Why do you want to ²._____ _____?
Miki: Because ³._____ _____ important to improve my English. I want to work for a foreign company ⁴._____ graduation.
Paul: Are there any other reasons ⁵._____ _____ Australia?
Miki: Yes, I have ⁶._____ other reasons. ⁷._____, Australia is a wonderful country full of beautiful nature.
Paul: What is ⁸._____ _____ reason?
Miki: The second reason ⁹._____ _____ I don't like getting jet lag. There is only a one-hour time difference between Japan ¹⁰._____ Australia.
Paul: Oh, I see. ¹¹._____, Australia is a good choice.

NOTES
offer「提供する」 participate in ~「~に参加する」 improve「向上させる」
work for ~「~で働く」 foreign company「外資系企業」 graduation「卒業」
choose「選択する」 full of beautiful nature「美しい自然の豊かな」 jet lag「時差ボケ」
time difference「時差」 between A and B「AとBの間で」 choice「選択」

Let's Practice

完成したら、意見と理由を述べる表現を意識しながら、ペアになってディスカッションの練習をしましょう。

Unit 6　Discussion 1

Unit 7

Discussion 2

理由と度合いを示して
同意・反論しよう

Introduction

DL 26　CD 26

Yumi: I think that university students should work part-time.
Kenta: I disagree with you.
Yumi: Why do you disagree with me?
Kenta: Because they should concentrate on their studies.

NOTE
concentrate on ~「~に専念する」

　議論を円滑に進めるためには、相手の主張に対して単に同意・反対するだけではなく、その根拠・理由を述べることが重要です。また、同意や反対の程度に合わせた言い方を選ぶ必要があります。

同意する

程度[高]：I totally agree with you.　まったく賛成です。　　Exactly!　まさしくその通り。
程度[中]：I agree with you.　賛成です。　　I feel the same way.　同感です。
程度[低]：I mostly agree with your opinion, but ...　あなたの意見におおむね賛成ですが、~。

反対する

程度[高]：I strongly disagree with you.　まったく反対です。
程度[中]：I disagree with you.　反対です。　　I don't think so.　そうは思いません。
程度[低]：I don't really agree with your opinion, but ...
　　　　　　　　　　　　　　　　　あなたの意見にまったく反対ではないのですが、~。

Warm-up

Exercise 1

日本語に合わせて、空所にふさわしい語を書き入れ、英文を完成させましょう。

1. 大学生は、ボランティア活動をすべきだと思います。

    I _____ that university students _____ _____ volunteer activities.

2. 同感です。 I feel the _____ _____.

3. 私たちは、節電することが必要だと思います。

    I think that _____ _____ necessary for us _____ save electricity.

4. あなたの意見におおむね賛成ですが、電気を使うことを完全にやめることはできません。

    I _____ _____ with your opinion, _____ we cannot totally stop _____ electricity.

Exercise 2

クラスメイトとペアになり、以下の会話文の下線部を替え、相手の主張に強く同意・反対し、その理由を述べる練習をしましょう。

強く同意する

Taku: I think that <u>university students should study abroad</u>.
 Mai: I totally agree with you, because <u>it is important for us to experience different cultures</u>.

強く反対する

Taku: I think that <u>libraries should be open for 24 hours a day</u>.
 Mai: I strongly disagree with you, because <u>it is unsafe for us to go out alone in the middle of the night</u>.

NOTES
go out alone「一人で出歩く」 in the middle of the night「真夜中に」

Reading

Chen教授のコミュニケーション学概論の授業でディスカッションをしました。どのような内容だったのか、英文を読んで、確認しましょう。　DL 28　CD 28

　I think having a part-time job has both good points and bad points. One good point is that we can gain experience in society. This experience will give us a good chance to think about our future career. However, one bad point is that it can affect academic scores. Some students can't get up in the morning and don't attend classes. The reason is that they become too busy with their part-time jobs. If you are thinking of working, I think you should consider when, how long, and why you want to do a part-time job before you start it.

NOTES
gain「得る」　future career「将来の職業」　affect「影響する」　academic scores「学業成績」
attend「出席する」　consider「考える」

Important Expressions

本文に出てきた表現を使って、以下の英文を完成させましょう。

1. ペットを飼うことには良い側面と悪い側面があります。

   Having a pet _____ _____ good points and bad points.

2. 理由は、エネルギーを節約しない人がいるからです。

   The _____ is that some people don't _____ energy.

3. あなたは、留学したい時期・期間・理由を考えるべきです。

   You should consider _____, _____ long and
   _____ you want to study abroad.

Discussion

Listen to the Discussion

DL 29　CD 29

一人暮らしについてのShunとKateのディスカッションを聴き、空所にふさわしい語を書き入れましょう。

Shun: Do you enjoy ¹._____ _____?
Kate: Yes, I do. I can stay up late, watch my favorite programs on TV, and go to bed whenever I want to.
Shun: I ²._____ _____ with you, but I found bad points, too.
Kate: What are the bad points?
Shun: You have to do everything all by yourself. For example, you have to ³._____ your room, ⁴._____ shopping and ⁵._____ groceries, ⁶._____, and take out the garbage.
Kate: I ⁷._____ with you. Those are good points. I enjoy buying groceries and cooking for myself.
Shun: Then, how about this? You have to wake yourself up. It is very hard for me to do.
Kate: I ⁸._____ with you on that.
Shun: Anyway, it is important ⁹._____ _____ responsible when you live alone.
Kate: Exactly!

NOTES
stay up late「夜更かしする」　whenever I want to「いつでも私が好きな時に」
all by yourself「すべて自分自身で」　take out the garbage「ゴミ出しをする」
wake ~ up「～を起こす」　anyway「ともかく」　be responsible「責任をもつ」

Let's Practice

完成したら、相手の意見に同意・反対したり理由を述べたりする表現を意識しながら、ペアになってディスカッションの練習をしましょう。

Unit 7　Discussion 2

Unit 8

Presentation 1

プレゼンテーションの基本構造［出だしと結び］

Introduction

　プレゼンテーション (presentation) とは、話し手が聴き手に知識や情報を伝えることです。似たようなものにスピーチがありますが、両者の違いはどこにあるのでしょうか。

　スピーチは、感謝や思い、夢などを心を込めて相手に伝えることで、聴衆の感情に訴える要素が大きいと言えるでしょう。他方、プレゼンテーションは、説明や提案などを、説得力のあるデータや理由を提示しながら、相手の知性に訴えます。

　プレゼンテーションは、出だし（イントロダクション）、具体的な内容（ボディ）、結び（コンクルージョン）の3つの部分から構成されています。

　聴き手が理解しやすいように出だしで結びに触れてから、ボディ部を展開し、最後に再び出だしに戻って結びとする、サンドイッチ型のプレゼンテーションも多く見られますが、このテキストでは、よりシンプルなスタイルのプレゼンテーションも扱います。

▼プレゼンテーションの基本構造

・Today, I would like to talk about ...
・I talked about ... today.
・Thank you for listening to my presentation.

　本章では、特に、出だしと結びについて学んでいきます。

出だしの表現

Today, I would like to talk about ...　今日は…について話したいと思います。

Today, I am going to talk about ...　今日は…について話すことにします。

Today's topic is ...　今日のトピックは…です。

The purpose of my presentation is to talk about ...
　　　　　私のプレゼンテーションの目的は…について話すことです。

The subject [theme] of my presentation is ...
　　　　　私のプレゼンテーションの主題[テーマ]は…です。

結びの表現

I talked about ... today.　今日は…についてお話ししました。

That's all I have to say about ...　以上が…について話すことすべてです。

I would like to conclude [finish] my talk.　これで私の話を終わります。

Thank you for listening to my presentation.
　　　　　プレゼンテーションを聴いていただきありがとうございます。

Thank you for your attention.　ご静聴ありがとうございます。

Warm-up

Introductionの「出だしの表現」と「結びの表現」を参考にしながら、日本語に合わせて、[　]内の語句を並べ替え、英文を完成させましょう。

1. 今日のトピックは、私の好きなスポーツについてです。

[favorite sport / is / my / Today's / topic].

_____.

2. 今日は野球についてお話しました。

[about / baseball / I / talked / today].

_____.

3. 今日は私のある友だちについて話したいと思います。

Today, [a friend of mine / I / like to / talk about / would].
Today, _____.

4. 私のプレゼンテーションの目的は、インドのカレーについて話すことです。

[is to / my presentation / of / The purpose / talk about] Indian curry.

_____ Indian curry.

5. プレゼンテーションを聴いていただきありがとうございます。

[listening to / for / you / my presentation / Thank].

_____.

Presentation A

「出だしの表現」と「結びの表現」に注意して、写真に関するプレゼンテーションの原稿を読んで、後に続く問題に答えましょう。

　Today, I would like to talk about Shiga. Shiga is famous for Lake Biwa, the biggest lake in Japan. But that is not all it is famous for. There are other things that you can enjoy in Shiga.

　First, Shiga has some high mountains around Lake Biwa, such as Mount Hiei and the Hira Mountains. The view of the lake from the mountains is fantastic! Second, Shiga is famous for Omi beef. It tastes delicious and is one of the three top brands of beef in Japan. Lastly, Shiga has the fourth largest number of national treasures. The number of visitors to them is not as large as the number of visitors to Kyoto and Nara, so you can take your time when you are in Shiga.

　Thank you for listening to my presentation.

NOTES
view「眺め」　national treasures「国宝」

Exercise

1. 本文中の「出だしの表現」を使った1文を書き出してみましょう。

_____

2. 本文中の「結びの表現」を使った1文を書き出してみましょう。

_____

3. 出だしに含まれている情報を1つ、日本語で述べましょう。

_____について

4. ボディに含まれている情報を3つ、日本語で述べましょう。

(1) _____ について
(2) _____ について
(3) _____ について

Listen to the Presentation

「出だしの表現」と「結びの表現」を確認しながら、**Presentation A**の音声を聴きましょう。　DL 30　CD 30

Presentation B

写真に関するプレゼンテーションの原稿を読んで、後に続く問題に答えましょう。

A. _____

three interesting buildings in the Umeda area in Osaka.

First, please look at the big Ferris wheel in the top picture. It looks like it is behind the buildings. But it is on the top of one of them. Second, please look at the bottom left picture. Two towers share a roof with each other. Many foreign tourists like to visit it because the roof part looks like a floating garden. Third, please look at the unique roof in the bottom right picture. Osaka station is located under it. This is a very interesting building! You can visit all of three of these buildings in just a few hours!

B. _____

NOTES
Ferris wheel「観覧車」　share A with B「AをBと共有する」　floating garden「空中庭園」

Exercise

1. 以下の語句を、本文中の下線部 A と B に当てはまるよう正しく並べ替え、書き入れましょう。なお、冒頭の語も小文字で示しています。

下線部 A [of / is / presentation / the subject / my]

下線部 B [your / thank / attention / for / you]

2. **Introduction** で学習した「出だしの表現」「結びの表現」を使って、**1** で並べ替えた下線部 A と B を含む英文を、別の英文に書き換えましょう。

下線部 A

Today, _____

_____

下線部 B

That's _____

3. 3枚の写真についてプレゼンテーションで述べられていることを、それぞれ日本語でまとめましょう。

上の写真
ビルの屋上に _____ があること

左下の写真
２つのビルが _____ していること

右下の写真
屋根の下に _____ があること

Listen to the Presentation

「出だしの表現」と「結びの表現」を確認しながら、完成した **Presentation B** の音声を聴きましょう。

DL 31　CD 31

Unit 9

Presentation 2

プレゼンテーションの具体的な内容［ボディ］

Introduction

　ここでは、プレゼンテーションの具体的な内容（ボディ）を中心に学びます。
　ボディは、プレゼンテーションの一番中心となるところで、発表者が独自の見解を述べる重要箇所です。聴き手が理解しやすい流れで進めていくために、出だしのところで伝えたことを、順序立てて詳しく説明や補足を加えていく必要があります。あらかじめ言いたいことがいくつあるのか、どのような順番で伝えればいいのかを考えておくとよいでしょう。

　本章では、言いたい項目の数を知らせる表現や順番を示す表現を活用できることを目標にします。

言いたい項目の数を知らせる表現

I would like to say three things about ...　…について3つのことを言いたいと思います。
I have three things about ... to tell you.　…について言いたいことが3つあります。
I want to tell you two things.　2つ言いたいことがあります。

順番を示す表現

First, ... Second, ... And finally (lastly), ...　第一に…、第二に…、そして最後に…
First, ... Next, ... Then, ...　第一に…、次に…、それから…

Warm-up

以下の英文は、1つのまとまったパラグラフを5つのセンテンスに分けたものです。プレゼンテーションの基本構造に合うよう、イントロダクションに続くa～dの英文を並べ替えましょう。

1. Today, I'm going to talk about my hobbies. I would like to say three things about them.

   _____ → _____ → _____ → _____

   a. And finally, I listen to the radio in my free time.
   b. First, one of my hobbies is watching baseball games.
   c. Thank you for listening to my presentation.
   d. Second, I like to go to see movies on the weekends.

2. Today's topic is my university days. I have three things to tell you about my university days.

   _____ → _____ → _____ → _____

   a. Thank you for listening to my presentation.
   b. And finally, I studied international studies and English.
   c. Second, I belonged to the English club there.
   d. First, I rented an apartment near the university and started living alone.

3. The purpose of my presentation is to talk about how to cook this dish. I want to tell you three things about it.

   _____ → _____ → _____ → _____

   a. Then, pan-fry all the ingredients and be careful not to burn them.
   b. First, cut these vegetables and chicken.
   c. Thank you for your attention.
   d. Lastly, add this spice before serving.

Presentation A

「言いたい項目の数を知らせる表現」と「順番を示す表現」に注意して、表に関するプレゼンテーションの原稿を読んで、後に続く問題に答えましょう。

	Mon	Tue	Wed	Thu	Fri	Sat	Sun
1				Beginners Seminar 入門ゼミ		Part-time Job	Free Time
2	Sociology 社会学	English 英語	Economics 1 経済学1	Introductory French 仏語初級			
3			Bookkeeping 簿記	Economics 2 経済学2	English 英語		
4	Japanese Constitution 日本国憲法	Part-time Job		Environmental Science 環境科学	Public Finance 財政学		
5	Introductory French 仏語初級			Part-time Job			
	Club		Club		Club		

　Today, I would like to talk about my busiest day of the week. Please look at my timetable. You can see that Thursday is very busy for me. I would like to say three things about it.

　First, after my club activities on Wednesdays, I have to do much homework for my French and Economics classes, so I don't get enough sleep. Next, as you can see, I have to get up early on Thursday to take four classes. Then, I work part-time at a convenience store after school from 5:00 p.m. to 10:00 p.m. Because of a lack of sleep, many classes, and my part-time job, I am tired every Thursday.

　That's all I have to say about my busiest day of the week. Thank you for listening.

NOTES
because of ~「~のために」（理由）　lack「不足」

Exercise

1. 本文中の「言いたい項目の数を知らせる表現」を使った1文を書き出してみましょう。

2. 本文中の「順番を示す表現」を3語書き出してみましょう。

_____   _____   _____

3. ボディに含まれている3つの情報を、<u>本文の順番通りに</u>日本語で述べましょう。

(1) _____ について

(2) _____ について

(3) _____ について

Listen to the Presentation

「言いたい項目の数を知らせる表現」と「順番を示す表現」を確認しながら、
Presentation A の音声を聴きましょう。　　　　　DL 32　　CD 32

Presentation B

Presentation A と同じ表に関するプレゼンテーションの原稿を読んで、後に続く質問に答えましょう。

　　Today's topic is about how I spend every Friday. Please look at my timetable. I would ^A._____.
^X._____, I get up ^1._____ in the morning, because I am very ^2._____ on Thursdays. I have to leave home for university at about 11:30 a.m. ^Y._____, I take ^3._____ in the afternoon. They are "English" and "Public Finance." And ^Z._____, I do ^4._____ after school. I am in the brass band club. I practice playing the flute from 6:00 p.m. to 8:00 p.m. I come home at about 9:00 p.m.

　　This is how I spend my Fridays. Thank you for listening.

Exercise

Presentation B の英文を読んで、以下の質問に答えましょう。

1. 以下の語句を、本文中の<u>下線部 A</u> に当てはまるよう正しく並べ替え、書き入れましょう。

[to / three things / say / like / it / about]

2. 本文中の3つの下線部 X, Y, Z に当てはまる語を選択肢から選び、書き入れましょう。なお、冒頭の語も小文字で示しています。

lastly　　three　　second　　first　　one

3. 順番を示す表現と Timetable を参考にしながら、破線部1〜4に当てはまる語句を選択肢から選び、書き入れましょう。

busy and tired　　late　　club activities　　two classes

Listen to the Presentation

「言いたい項目の数を知らせる表現」と「順番を示す表現」を確認しながら、完成した **Presentation B** の音声を聴きましょう。　　　　DL 33　　CD 33

Let's Try!

Presentation B を参考に、以下のフォーマットを使って、自分の授業のある曜日を紹介してみましょう。

　　Today's topic is about how I spend every _____ 曜日. Please look at my timetable. I would like to say three things about it.

　　First, I get up at _____ 時間. Second, I take _____ 授業数 class(es). They are [It is] _____ 授業名. And lastly, I _____ 授業後に〜をする after school from _____ 時間 to _____ 時間.

　　This is how I spend _____ 曜日（複数形）. Thank you for listening.

Unit 10

Presentation 3

グラフを使った
プレゼンテーション

Introduction

　プレゼンテーションでは、資料を提示しながら進めていく場合がよくあります。グラフなどを用いることで、聴き手の理解も増し、より説得力のあるプレゼンテーションを展開することができます。いくつかグラフの種類を紹介しましょう。

・円グラフ［pie chart］
　ある項目が、全体（100%）の中でどれ位の割合を占めているかを示す時に使用します。

・棒グラフ［bar graph］
　項目同士を比較する時や、ある項目に関して、「2つの時期」や「男性と女性」、「10代、20代、30代の回答の差」など、複数の観点を示す時に使用します。

・折れ線グラフ［line graph］
　時系列に見た変動を示す際に使用すると便利なグラフです。

　本章では、特に、円グラフを使ったプレゼンテーションについて学んでいきます。

▶ グラフや数値を提示する時の表現

The pie chart [bar graph] is about ...　円グラフ［棒グラフ］は…についてのものです。

This section shows ...　この部分は…を示しています。

The "A" section occupies ... % of the chart.　「A」の部分がグラフの…%を占めています。

▶ 注目を求める時の表現

Please look at ...　…をご覧ください。

Let's look at the graph.　グラフをご覧ください。

As you can see, ...　ご覧のように…

Warm-up

Introductionで学んだ表現を参考にして、空所にふさわしい語を書き入れ、英文を完成させましょう。

1. 円グラフをご覧ください。
   Let's look at the _____ _____.

2. このグラフは小学生の好きなスポーツについてのものです。
   This graph _____ _____ elementary school children's favorite sports.

3. ご覧のように、彼らはフィギュアスケートが最も好きです。
   _____ _____ _____ _____, they like figure skating the best.

4. 「野球」の部分を見てください。それはグラフの 26% を占めています。
   Please look at the "baseball" _____. It _____ 26% of the chart.

Presentation A

「グラフや数値を提示する時の表現」と「注目を求める時の表現」に注意して、円グラフに関するプレゼンテーションの原稿を読んで、後に続く問題に答えましょう。

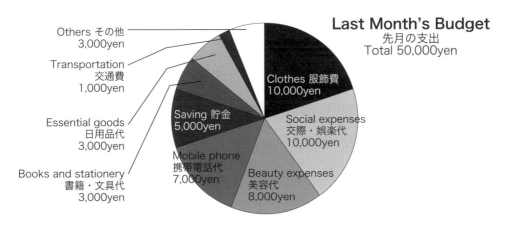

Today, I would like to talk about my pocket money.

This pie chart shows how I used my money last month. I made 50,000 yen at my part-time job. First, please look at the section "social expenses." As you can see, it occupies 20% of the total. I use this money to eat out a couple of times a month and go to karaoke with my friends. Second, please look at the section "beauty expenses." The section is larger than usual, because I had a haircut last month. And finally, please look at the section "books and stationery." I often read books when I am on the train. I buy three or four books every month. This section shows that I spent 3,000 yen last month.

Thank you for your attention.

Exercise

1. 本文中の「グラフを提示する時の表現」を使った1文を書き出してみましょう。

_____

2. 本文中の「注目を求める時の表現」を使った語句を書き出してみましょう。

_____

3. ボディに含まれている3つの情報を、本文の順番通りに日本語で述べましょう。
　　(1) _____ について
　　(2) _____ について
　　(3) _____ について

Listen to the Presentation

「グラフや数値を提示する時の表現」と「注目を求める時の表現」を確認しながら、
Presentation Aの音声を聴きましょう。　　　　　　DL 34　　CD 34

Presentation B

円グラフに関するプレゼンテーションの原稿を読んで、後に続く問題に答えましょう。

The topic of today's presentation is how students in Kyoto go to school. I asked students at Kiyomizu University about it. ^A._____

_____.

^1._____, please look at the section called "By bicycle." As you can see, about one in three students goes to school by bicycle. The number of the bicycle users in Kyoto is the largest in Japan. ^2._____, please look at the section called " ^X._____." There is a subway station near Kiyomizu University. Many students live far from the university, so they go to school ^X._____. And ^3._____, please look at the section called " ^Y._____." For the students at Kiyomizu University, the bus is convenient because the campus is on a hill. It is hard to walk to the university.

Thank you for listening to my presentation.

NOTES
about one in three students「約3人の学生のうち1人」 the number of ~「〜の数」
bicycle user「自転車の利用者」 on a hill「丘の上に」

Exercise

1. 以下の語句を、本文中の下線部 A に当てはまるよう正しく並べ替え、書き入れましょう。なお、冒頭の語も小文字で示しています。

   [about / is / pie chart / these results / this]

2. 本文中の破線部 1 〜 3 に当てはまる語を選択肢から選び、書き入れましょう。なお、冒頭の語も小文字で示しています。

   finally　　first　　one　　second　　three

3. 本文中の下線部 X と Y に当てはまる語を、グラフなどを参考にして書き入れましょう。

Listen to the Presentation

「グラフや数値を提示する時の表現」と「注目を求める時の表現」を確認しながら、完成した **Presentation B** の音声を聴きましょう。　　DL 35　　CD 35

Let's Try!

以下の円グラフは、Nakasu High Schoolの生徒が最も使う交通手段が、徒歩（On foot）、自転車（By bicycle）、電車（By train）、バス（By bus）、その他（Others）のうちどれかを調査し、まとめたものです。
Presentation B を参考にして、円グラフについて、英語で説明してみましょう。

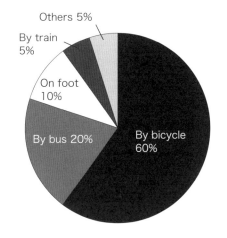

1. Please look at the "By bicycle" section. It is ＿＿＿＿ 数字 %. Many students go to school by ＿＿＿＿＿＿＿＿＿ 交通手段 .

2. Please look at the "By bus" section. It is only ＿＿＿＿ 数字 %. Some students go to school by ＿＿＿＿＿＿＿＿＿ 交通手段 .

3. Please look at the "By train" section. It is only ＿＿＿＿ 数字 %. Few students go to school by ＿＿＿＿＿＿＿＿＿ 交通手段 .

ディベート (debate) について

ディベートとは？

　ディベートは、ある論題（proposition）について肯定側（affirmative side）と否定側（negative side）の２つのチームに分かれて、ルールに従い、スピーチを行う論戦です。肯定側と否定側のどちらのチームになるかは抽選などによって決められ、ゲームに参加します。また、自分の立場に沿った意見のみをスピーチするのではなく、対立するチームの議論に対して反論したり、自分のチームの議論と比較をしたりすることが大切です。

ディスカッションとの違い

　Unit 6, 7で学習したディスカッションと似ていますが、ディスカッションは自分と対立する相手との意思統一を図る言語活動であるのに対し、ディベートは第三者である聴衆（audience）を説得する「ことばのゲーム」です。聴衆が両チームのスピーチの優劣を判定し、勝敗が決まります。

ディベートの構成

　ディベートは立論（constructive speech）と反駁（rebuttal speech）というスピーチによって構成されます。立論とは、「論題について自分たちのチームの意見を理由や例を挙げながら述べるスピーチ」のことであり、反駁（本テキストでは「反論」）とは、「相手の立論に対して反論を行うスピーチ」のことです。ディベートは８分間の立論と５分間の反駁のスピーチを両チームともにそれぞれ複数回行います。

シンプル・ディベート

　このテキストでは、従来のディベートのスピーチ時間およびスピーチ回数を短縮した「シンプル・ディベート（simplified debate）」と呼ばれる形式のディベートを行います。簡潔な英語を用いてディベートを行うことにより、自分個人の意見に留まらず、物事を多角的・批判的に捉え、それを英語で伝えるという練習を行っていきましょう。

シンプル・ディベートの進め方

- 特定の論題について肯定側（affirmative side）と否定側（negative side）のチームに分かれます。それぞれ２人１組でチームを組みます。
- 各チームで、立論・反論のスピーチを１人１回担当するように役割分担を行います。スピーカー１人あたり、１回のスピーチはそれぞれ１分以内で行うものとします。聴衆の中の１人がタイム・キーパーを務め、スピーチの時間管理を行います。
- 対戦する２つのチームは、まず自分のチームの立論を作成し、事前にお互いの立論を交換します。反論の際、相手チームにどのように反論するか考えておくと、スムーズに反論が行えます。

Unit 11

Simplified Debate 1

主張の理由や具体例を示す

Introduction

以下の２つの文からどういう情報が読み取れますか。

Ryota is very funny.　　　　　　リョウタはとても面白い。

Kana likes to listen to music.　　カナは音楽を聴くのが好きだ。

リョウタはどういったところが面白いのでしょうか。カナは実際どんな音楽を聴くのでしょうか。以下のように、下線部の情報を加えると、面白い理由や好きな音楽の例が明確になり、具体的でわかりやすい文章になります。

Ryota is very funny *because* he always makes jokes.

　　　　　リョウタはとても面白い。なぜなら、彼はいつもジョークを言うから。

Kana likes to listen to music. *For example,* she really loves pop music.

　　　　　カナは音楽を聴くのが好きだ。例えば、彼女はポップ・ミュージックが大好きだ。

このように、becauseのような理由を示す表現や、for exampleのような具体例を示す表現を身につけることは、スピーチの活動にとって重要です。

理由や具体例を示す表現

because ...　なぜなら…　　　　... for the following three reasons　以下の３つの理由で…
First, ... Second, ... And finally (lastly), ...　第一に…、第二に…、そして最後に…
For example, / For instance, / such as　例えば
So, ... / Therefore, ... / For these reasons, ...　だから…

シンプル・ディベート（simplified debate）では、まず、肯定チームと否定チームがテーマに対して意見を述べる立論を行います。この章では、スピーチが聴き手にとってより論理的でわかりやすいものになるように、理由や具体例を示す表現を学びます。これらの表現を用いれば、どのようなテーマに対しても、次ページのテンプレートに従って立論ができます。

立論のスピーチのテンプレート

	①チームで主張したいこと	for the following two reasons.
First,	②主張したい理由 (1)	
For example,	③その具体例 (1)	
Second,	④主張したい理由 (2)	
For instance,	⑤その具体例 (2)	
Therefore,	⑥まとめ	

Warm-up

日本語に合わせて空所にふさわしい語を書き入れ、英文を完成させましょう。

1. 私はいろいろなスポーツをするのが好きです。例えば、野球は好きなスポーツの一つです。

I like to play many kinds of sports. _____ _____, baseball is one of my favorite sports.

2. あのレストランは、以下の２つの理由でとても人気があります。第一に、料理がおいしいです。第二に、価格がお手頃です。

That restaurant is very popular for the following two reasons. _____, the dishes are delicious. _____, the price is reasonable.

NOTES
dish「料理」 price「価格」 reasonable「手頃な」

3. 私は、以下の３つの理由でネットショッピングが好きです。初めに、私が欲しいものをいつでも注文できるからです。２つ目に、服やCD、本などの多くの種類の商品を検索することができるからです。最後に、探している商品についての他の客のレビューを見ることができるからです。よって、私はインターネットで買い物をするのはよいことだと思います。

I like online shopping for the following three reasons. _____, I can order what I want anytime. Second, I can search for many kinds of goods _____ _____ clothes, CDs, and books. _____, I can see other customers' reviews of the goods that I'm looking at. _____, I think it is good to do my shopping on the Internet.

NOTES
online shopping「ネットショッピング」 order「〜を注文する」 goods「商品」
what I want「私が欲しいもの」 anytime「いつでも」 search for 〜「〜を検索する」
other customers「他の客」 review「レビュー」

Unit 11　Simplified Debate 1

Simplified Debate A

以下の英文は、1つのまとまったパラグラフを複数のセンテンスに分けたものです。意味が通るようにこれらの英文を並べ替えましょう。なお、**a**の位置については各問題で固定しています。

1. a → _____ → _____ → _____ → _____

    a. Using the Internet has many advantages.
    b. First, there is a lot of information on the Internet.
    c. Finally, we can communicate with many friends.
    d. Second, we can get information anytime.
    e. Therefore, the Internet is a very useful tool for us.

NOTES
information「情報」 communicate with ~「~とコミュニケーションをとる」
useful「役に立つ」 tool「道具」

2. _____ → _____ → a → _____ → _____

    a. For instance, I go to the Gion Festival with my friends.
    b. For two reasons, my favorite season of the year is summer.
    c. Therefore, I like summer the best of all seasons.
    d. Second, the food such as shaved ice and *soumen* is very delicious.
    e. First, I can enjoy many festivals every summer.

NOTES
festival「祭り」 favorite season of the year「1年で好きな季節」
of all seasons「すべての季節の中で」 shaved ice「カキ氷」

3. _____ → _____ → _____ → _____ → _____ → a

    a. Therefore, children should not play video games.
    b. Playing video games is bad for children's health for the following two reasons.
    c. For example, they stay home for a long time, and don't play with their friends outside.
    d. First, they don't get enough exercise.
    e. Second, playing games is bad for their eyes.
    f. For instance, the light from the screen can damage their eyes.

NOTES
health「健康」 stay home「家にいる」 for a long time「長時間」 outside「外で」
get enough exercise「十分な運動を行う」 damage「痛める」

48

Simplified Debate B

「ファストフードを食べるのは良いことである」というテーマで、肯定チームと否定チームに分かれ、シンプル・ディベートを行います。以下の英文は肯定チームの立論のスピーチの一部です。スピーチの原稿を読んで、後に続く問題に答えましょう。

　We think that eating fast food is good for the following two reasons. ^A._____, we can save time by eating fast food when we are busy. For example, fast food restaurants can quickly serve us our food after we order it. ^B._____, fast food is not so expensive. ^C._____, we can eat *gyudon* for about 400 yen at a *gyudon* shop. Therefore, eating fast food has many advantages.

NOTES
save time「時間を節約する」　serve A B「AにBを出す」

Exercise

1. 本文中の「ファストフードを食べるのは良いことである」とする理由の数を知らせる1文を書き出してみましょう。

   _____

2. 本文中の3つの下線部 A, B, C に当てはまる語を以下の選択肢から選び、書き入れましょう。なお、冒頭の語も小文字で示しています。

   first　　such as　　for instance　　lastly　　second

3. 「ファストフードを食べるのは良い」とする理由について、日本語で述べましょう。

   1つ目は、_____ こと。
   例えば、_____

   2つ目は、_____ こと。
   例えば、_____

Listen to the Simplified Debate

理由や具体例を示す表現を確認しながら、完成した**Simplified Debate B**の原稿の音声を聴きましょう。

DL 36　　CD 36

Simplified Debate C

以下の英文は、「ファストフードを食べるのは良いことである」というテーマのシンプル・ディベートにおける、否定チームの立論のスピーチの一部です。スピーチの原稿を読んで、後に続く問題に答えましょう。

　　We think that ^X.＿＿＿＿＿＿＿＿＿＿＿＿＿＿＿＿＿＿＿＿＿＿＿＿＿＿＿＿＿＿＿＿＿. First, we might gain weight if we eat too much fast food. ^A.＿＿＿＿＿＿＿＿＿, we can consume more than 300 kilocalories per cheeseburger. ^B.＿＿＿＿＿＿＿, we eat fewer vegetables if we eat at fast food restaurants. For instance, we eat only a few slices of onions at *gyudon* restaurants. ^C.＿＿＿＿＿＿＿, eating fast food has many ^D.＿＿＿＿＿＿.

NOTES
　gain weight「太る」　consume more than 300 kilocalories「300キロカロリー以上摂る」
　per cheeseburger「チーズバーガー1個につき」

Exercise

1. 以下の語句を、本文中の下線部 X に当てはまるよう正しく並べ替え、書き入れましょう。

[eating / fast food / following / for the / is bad / two reasons]

2. 本文中の4つの下線部 A〜D に当てはまる語を以下の選択肢から選び、書き入れましょう。なお、冒頭の語も小文字で示しています。

advantages　　disadvantages　　for example　　for these reasons
lastly　　second　　therefore

3. 「ファストフードを食べるのは悪い」とする理由について、日本語で述べましょう。

　1つ目は、＿＿＿＿＿＿＿＿＿＿＿＿＿＿＿＿＿＿＿＿＿＿＿＿＿＿＿＿こと。
　例えば、＿＿＿＿＿＿＿＿＿＿＿＿＿＿＿＿＿＿＿＿＿＿＿＿＿＿＿＿＿＿
　2つ目は、＿＿＿＿＿＿＿＿＿＿＿＿＿＿＿＿＿＿＿＿＿＿＿＿＿＿＿＿こと。
　例えば、＿＿＿＿＿＿＿＿＿＿＿＿＿＿＿＿＿＿＿＿＿＿＿＿＿＿＿＿＿＿

Listen to the Simplified Debate

理由や具体例を示す表現を確認しながら、完成した **Simplified Debate C** の原稿の音声を聴きましょう。

Unit 12

Simplified Debate 2

理由や具体例を示して立論する

Introduction

　人に何かを主張する時は、その理由や具体例を提示することが重要です。
　Using the Internet is good.　インターネットを使うのは良いことだ。
と主張したければ、なぜインターネットを使うのが良いことなのか、理由を提示する必要があります。そして、具体例を挙げると、よりスピーチが魅力的になるでしょう。
　We can get a lot of information on the Internet.
　　　　　インターネットで多くの情報が得られる。
　For example, we can know the latest news.
　　　　　例えば、最新のニュースを知ることができる。
さらに、インターネットを使うことの良い点を複数挙げられると、より主張したいことの説得力が増します。
　There are many fun websites on the Internet.
　　　　　インターネットには多くの楽しいサイトがある。
　For instance, we can enjoy watching movies for free.
　　　　　例えば、無料で動画を見るのを楽しむことができる。
　このように、本章では、前章で紹介した「立論のスピーチのテンプレート」を用いて作る立論の内容について学びます。

立論のスピーチのテンプレート

	①チームで主張したいこと	for the following two reasons.
First,	②主張したい理由 (1)	
For example,	③その具体例 (1)	
Second,	④主張したい理由 (2)	
For instance,	⑤その具体例 (2)	
Therefore,	⑥まとめ	

Warm-up

「インターネットを使うのは良いことである」というテーマで、シンプル・ディベートを行います。肯定チームの立論のスピーチを作りましょう。テンプレートを用いる前に、チャートで主張・理由・具体例を組み立てていくと良いでしょう。

Exercise 1

Introductionを参考に、[　]内に日本語と英語のキーワードを書き入れましょう。

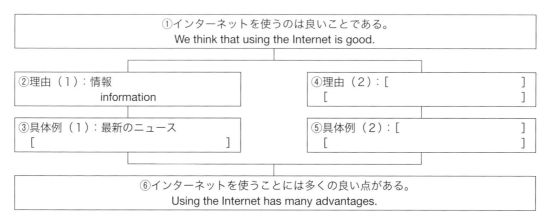

①インターネットを使うのは良いことである。
We think that using the Internet is good.

②理由（1）：情報
information

④理由（2）：[　　　　　]
[　　　　　]

③具体例（1）：最新のニュース
[　　　　　]

⑤具体例（2）：[　　　　　]
[　　　　　]

⑥インターネットを使うことには多くの良い点がある。
Using the Internet has many advantages.

Exercise 2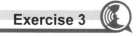

肯定チームの立論を、テンプレートを用いて作ってみましょう。**Introduction**の英文と**Exercise 1**のキーワードを参考にして、②〜⑤に入る文章を作りましょう。

① We think that using the Internet is good for the following two reasons.

First, ②

For example, ③

Second, ④

For instance, ⑤

⑥ Therefore, using the Internet has many advantages.

Exercise 3

他にもキーワードを考えて、理由や具体例を英語で述べる練習をしましょう。

「田舎より都会に住む方が良い」というテーマでシンプル・ディベートを行います。以下のSimplified Debate A～Cの流れで、肯定チームと否定チームの立論を作成しましょう。

Simplified Debate A

Exercise 1

以下の英文は、都会あるいは田舎に住む上での利点を述べたものです。それぞれ都会と田舎のどちらについての英文か考え、空所にcityあるいはcountrysideを書き入れましょう。

a. There are a lot of transportation options in the _____.
b. We can live a quiet life in the _____.
c. There are many fun events in the _____.
d. We can eat a lot of fresh food in the _____.
e. The _____ has a lot of nature.
f. Living in the _____ is convenient.

NOTE
transportation「交通機関」

Exercise 2

以下の語句は、立論する上で必要なキーワードです。それぞれの語句が、Exercise 1のどの英文と関係のあるキーワードか考え、a～fの記号で答えましょう。

1. many buses   [   ]
2. clean air   [   ]
3. concerts   [   ]
4. fresh vegetables [   ]
5. mountains   [   ]
6. movie theaters   [   ]
7. nice restaurants [   ]
8. few trains   [   ]
9. river   [   ]
10. shopping centers [   ]
11. fruit farm   [   ]
12. subway   [   ]
13. lake   [   ]
14. sporting events [   ]
15. theme parks   [   ]

Simplified Debate B

「都会に住むこと」について述べた英文を読んで、後に続く問題に答えましょう。

DL 38　CD 38

　　There are many advantages to living in the city. First, it is convenient to live in the city. For example, we can easily go to many shopping centers, movie theaters, and theme parks. Second, there are many activities for people to do. For instance, there are sporting events, plays and concerts all the year round. Lastly, we can travel to other cities quite easily. Most big cities have airports and large train stations, so it is easy for us to visit different parts of the country.

NOTE
　all the year round「一年中」

Exercise 1

「都会に住むこと」の利点と具体例を、それぞれ3つ日本語で述べましょう。

　　　１つ目は、＿＿＿＿＿＿＿＿＿＿＿＿＿＿＿＿＿＿＿＿＿＿＿＿＿＿＿こと。
　　　例えば、＿＿＿＿＿＿＿＿＿＿＿＿＿＿＿＿＿＿＿＿＿＿＿＿＿＿＿＿＿
　　　２つ目は、＿＿＿＿＿＿＿＿＿＿＿＿＿＿＿＿＿＿＿＿＿＿＿＿＿＿＿こと。
　　　例えば、＿＿＿＿＿＿＿＿＿＿＿＿＿＿＿＿＿＿＿＿＿＿＿＿＿＿＿＿＿
　　　３つ目は、＿＿＿＿＿＿＿＿＿＿＿＿＿＿＿＿＿＿＿＿＿＿＿＿＿＿＿こと。
　　　例えば、＿＿＿＿＿＿＿＿＿＿＿＿＿＿＿＿＿＿＿＿＿＿＿＿＿＿＿＿＿

Exercise 2

肯定チームの立論を、テンプレートを用いて完成させましょう。**Exercise 1**や**Simplified Debate A**の内容を参考にして、②～⑤に入る文章を作りましょう。

① We think that living in the city is good for the following two reasons.

　　First, ②＿＿＿＿＿＿＿＿＿＿＿＿＿＿＿＿＿＿＿＿＿＿＿＿＿＿＿

　　For example, ③＿＿＿＿＿＿＿＿＿＿＿＿＿＿＿＿＿＿＿＿＿＿＿＿

　　Second, ④＿＿＿＿＿＿＿＿＿＿＿＿＿＿＿＿＿＿＿＿＿＿＿＿＿＿

　　For instance, ⑤＿＿＿＿＿＿＿＿＿＿＿＿＿＿＿＿＿＿＿＿＿＿＿

⑥ Therefore, living in the city has many advantages.

Simplified Debate C

「田舎に住むこと」について述べた英文を読んで、後に続く問題に答えましょう。

DL 39　CD 39

　　Living in the countryside has many advantages. First, we can see and feel nature when living in the countryside. For example, we can always see the mountains and be close to rivers and lakes. Next, fresh food is always available to us when we live in the countryside. For instance, the many fields around the houses are often full of fresh fruit and vegetables during all seasons. Finally, we can live a quiet life. There are not many cars, trains, buses or airports when we live in the countryside.

NOTES
available「手に入る」　field「畑」

Exercise 1

「田舎に住むこと」の利点と具体例を、それぞれ３つ日本語で述べましょう。

１つ目は、_____こと。
例えば、_____
２つ目は、_____こと。
例えば、_____
３つ目は、_____こと。
例えば、_____

Exercise 2

否定チームの立論を、テンプレートを用いて完成させましょう。**Exercise 1**や**Simplified Debate A**の内容を参考にして、②〜⑤に入る文章を作りましょう。

① We think that living in the countryside is good for the following two reasons.

First, ②

For example, ③

Second, ④

For instance, ⑤

⑥ Therefore, living in the countryside has many advantages.

Unit 13

Simplified Debate 3

相手の立論に反論する

Introduction

　前章までは、シンプル・ディベートにおいて自分たちの「立論」を述べる際の表現や「立論」の内容について学びました。しかし、ディベートでは、自分たちの立場で意見を述べるだけでなく、相手の立場に立って考え、相手の情報に「反論」もしなければなりません。

あるテーマについて、肯定チームと否定チームに分かれシンプル・ディベートを行う場合

①肯定チームの立論 ⇒ ②否定チームの立論
　　　　　　　　　　　　　　　↓
④否定チームへの反論(肯定チームによる) ⇐ ③肯定チームへの反論(否定チームによる)

　反論は、まず反論のポイントがいくつあるのかを聴いている人たちに伝え、次に、相手のどの意見に反論するのかを確認してから反論すると、聴き手にとって非常に理解しやすくなります。

▶ 反論の出だしの表現

We would like to say two things about their opinions.
　　　　　　　　　　　　　彼らの意見について2つ言いたいことがあります。

We have three things to say about their opinions.
　　　　　　　　　　　　　彼らの意見について言うべきことが3つあります。

▶ 相手の意見の確認とそれに対する反論を行う際の表現

First, they said that _____. But we don't agree because ...
　　　1つ目に、彼らは_____と言いました。しかし、それには同意しません。なぜなら…

Second, they said that _____. But we also disagree with this idea because ...
　　　2つ目に、彼らは_____と言いました。しかし、それにも反対します。なぜなら…

反論の結びの表現

Therefore, we don't agree with their opinions.　よって、彼らの意見に同意しません。

これらの反論における表現を用いれば、どのような立論に対しても、以下のテンプレートに従って反論ができます。

反論のスピーチのテンプレート

We would like to say two things about their opinions.
First, they said that 　①相手チームの1つ目の立論　.
But we don't agree because 　②①に対する反論　.
Second, they said that 　③相手チームの2つ目の立論　.
We also disagree with this idea because 　④③に対する反論　.
Therefore, we don't agree with their opinions. / So, we disagree with their opinions.

Warm-up

日本語に合わせて、[　]内の語句を並べ替え、英文を完成させましょう。

1. 私たちは、ジェームズの意見について言いたいことが1つあります。

   We would [about / James's opinion / like to / say / one thing].
   We would _____.

2. 彼は、私たちはインターネットを利用するべきではないと言いました。

   He [said that / should not / the Internet / use / we].
   He _____.

3. しかし、それに同意しません。なぜなら、インターネットなしで生活するのは大変だからです。

   But [because / don't agree / it is / to live without the Internet / very hard / we].
   But _____.

4. だから、私たちは彼の意見には反対です。

   [disagree / opinion / Therefore, / his / we / with]

   _____.

Unit 13　Simplified Debate 3

Simplified Debate A

以下は、「インターネットを使うのは良いことである」というテーマでシンプル・ディベートを行った際の、肯定チームの立論における主張です。

肯定チーム

1. We can quickly get a lot of information on the Internet.
   私たちは、インターネット上でたくさんの情報をすぐに入手できる。
2. We can communicate with our friends on the Internet.
   私たちは、インターネット上で友だちとコミュニケーションをとることができる。

一方以下は、肯定チームの2つの主張に対する、否定チームとしての反論です。**Introduction**で学んだ表現を参考にして、空所に語句や文を書き入れ、反論のスピーチを完成させましょう。

DL 40　CD 40

We would like to say two things about their opinions.

First, they said that _____
_____.

But _____ because we can also get a lot of incorrect information on the Internet.

Second, they said that _____
_____.

However, _____ because we can also talk with them on the phone.

Therefore, we don't agree with their opinions.

否定チーム

Simplified Debate B

以下は、「ファストフードを食べるのは良いことである」というテーマでシンプル・ディベートを行った際の、肯定チームの立論のスピーチです。英文を読んで、後に続く問題に答えましょう。

We think that eating fast food is good for the following two reasons. First, we can save time by eating fast food when we are busy. For example, fast food restaurants can quickly serve us our food after we order it. Second, fast food is not so expensive. For instance, we can eat *gyudon* for about 400 yen at a *gyudon* shop. Therefore, eating fast food has many advantages.

Exercise

否定チームは、肯定チームの主張に対して、以下のように反論しています。

_____. First, they said that _____. But _____ because we should take our time when eating. It is important to slowly eat a meal even if we are busy. Second, they said that _____. However, _____ because fast food itself is quite expensive. Therefore, we don't agree with their opinions.

1. 空所に語句や文を書き入れ、反論のスピーチを完成させましょう。
2. 否定チームは、肯定チームの2つの主張に対して、どのように反論していますか。日本語で簡潔に述べましょう。

    肯定チームの立論①：ファストフードを食べることによって、時間を節約できる。
    否定チームの反論：_____

    肯定チームの立論②：ファストフードは値段が高くない。
    否定チームの反論：_____

Listen to the Simplified Debate

立論と反論の表現を確認しながら、完成したSimplified Debate Bの2つの音声を聴きましょう。

Simplified Debate C

以下は、「ファストフードを食べるのは良いことである」というテーマでシンプル・ディベートを行った際の、否定チームの立論のスピーチです。英文を読んで、後に続く問題に答えましょう。

　　We think that eating fast food is bad for the following two reasons. First, we might gain weight if we eat too much fast food. For example, we can consume more than 300 kilocalories per cheeseburger. Second, we eat fewer vegetables if we eat at fast food restaurants. For instance, we eat only a few slices of onions at *gyudon* restaurants. Therefore, eating fast food has many disadvantages.

Exercise

肯定チームは、否定チームの主張に対して、以下のように反論しています。

_____. First, they said that _____. But _____ because if we get enough exercise, we can eat whatever we want. Second, they said that _____. However, _____ because some restaurants serve salad and we can eat many kinds of vegetables there. Therefore, we don't agree with their opinions.

1. 空所に語句や文を書き入れ、反論のスピーチを完成させましょう。

2. 肯定チームは、否定チームの2つの主張に対して、どのように反論していますか。日本語で簡潔に述べましょう。

   否定チームの立論①：ファストフードを食べすぎると太ってしまうかもしれない。
   肯定のチーム反論：_____

   否定チームの立論②：ファストフードは野菜を十分に摂ることができない。
   肯定チームの反論：_____

Listen to the Simplified Debate

立論と反論の表現を確認しながら、完成したSimplified Debate Cの2つの音声を聴きましょう。

Unit 14

Simplified Debate 4

立場や見方を変えて
反論を発想する

Introduction

　現代は、インターネットの普及により、たくさんの情報に素早くアクセスできる便利な時代です。しかし、たくさんの情報が手に入る時代だからこそ、私たちは一つひとつの情報が正しいのか、重要なのかを「批判的に見る力」を養う必要があります。

　前章では、対立する立場の意見に反論するための方法・表現を学びました。本章では、それぞれの反論をどのように発想し、英語で表現するのか具体的に考えていきます。

　以下は、「インターネットを使うのは良いことである」というテーマでシンプル・ディベートを行う際の、肯定チームの立論です。

立論1. We can quickly get a lot of information on the Internet.
　　　私たちは、インターネット上でたくさんの情報をすぐに入手できる。

立論2. There are many fun websites on the Internet.
　　　インターネット上には楽しいサイトがたくさんある。

　以下は肯定チームのそれぞれの立論に対する、否定チームの反論です。

反論1. ... there is also a lot of incorrect information on the Internet.

反論2. ... young people usually stay awake late at night to look at these websites.

　反論1は「インターネット上には有益な情報だけでなく、不正確な情報もたくさんある」、反論2は「楽しいサイトを見るのに熱中して、夜更かししてしまう」という主張です。これらは、メリットから悪いことが生じるという反論の考え方です。

　その他の考え方として、以下のような反論方法もあります。

反論1-2. We can get information by reading newspapers and watching TV.

　これは、立論1に対して、「新聞を読んだりテレビを見たりすることで、情報を得ることができる」といった反論で、肯定チームが提示したメリットは他の方法でも得られるため重要ではないという考え方です。

このように、立場や見方を変えることで同じ事柄でも違った側面があるとわかります。反論のテンプレートを用いて、それらを英語で表現する練習をしていきましょう。

反論のスピーチのテンプレート

We would like to say two things about their opinions.
First, they said that ①相手チームの１つ目の立論 .
But we don't agree because ②①に対する反論 .
Second, they said that ③相手チームの２つ目の立論 .
We also disagree with this idea because ④③に対する反論 .
Therefore, we don't agree with their opinions. / So, we disagree with their opinions.

Warm-up

以下は、「インターネットを使うのは良いことである」というテーマでシンプル・ディベートを行った際の、肯定チームの立論における主張の一部です。 DL 45　CD 45

肯定チーム

We think that using the Internet is good for the following two reasons. First, we can quickly get a lot of information on the Internet. For example, we can quickly know the latest news by using our own computer and mobile phone. Second .... Therefore, using the Internet has many advantages.

一方、以下は、否定チームの反論の一部です。**Introduction**で学んだ表現を参考にして、空所に語句や文を書き入れ、反論のスピーチを完成させましょう。 DL 46　CD 46

We would like to say two things about their opinions.
First, they said that ＿＿＿＿＿＿＿＿＿＿＿＿＿＿＿＿＿＿＿＿＿＿＿＿＿＿＿＿＿＿＿＿ .
But we don't agree because ＿＿＿＿＿＿＿＿＿＿＿＿＿＿＿＿＿＿＿＿＿＿＿＿＿＿＿＿＿＿ .
Second .... Therefore, we don't agree with their opinions.

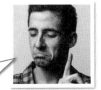

否定チーム

Simplified Debate A

「田舎よりも都会に住む方が良い」というテーマでシンプル・ディベートを行う際の、反論の発想について考えます。

Exercise 1

以下の語句は、反論する上で必要なキーワードです。それぞれの語句について、都会の生活と関連していると思われる場合はAを、田舎の生活と関連していると思われる場合はBを選びましょう。

1. crowded　　　　　　　[A / B]
2. high prices　　　　　　[A / B]
3. little transportation　　[A / B]
4. traffic accidents　　　　[A / B]
5. wild animals　　　　　　[A / B]

Exercise 2

以下の英文は、都会あるいは田舎に住む上でのデメリットを述べたものです。それぞれ都会と田舎のどちらについての英文かを考え、**Exercise 1**のキーワードを参考にして、空所に相応しい単語を書き入れましょう。

1. There are many cars around shopping centers, so we might be involved in _____ _____.
2. The _____ in the city are quite high, so it is hard for us to make a living there.
3. Large train stations are quite _____, and it is stressful.
4. There are many _____ _____ in the countryside, and they sometimes invade people's homes and farms.
5. It is inconvenient to live in the countryside if there is not much _____.

NOTES
be involved in ~「~に巻きこまれる」　make a living「生計を立てる」
stressful「ストレスの多い」　invade ~「~に入りこむ・侵入する」　inconvenient「不便な」

Simplified Debate B

以下は、「田舎よりも都会に住む方が良い」というテーマでシンプル・ディベートを行った際の、肯定チームあるいは否定チームの立論の一部です。前章で学んだ表現や [Hints] の内容を参考にして、ペアになって反論の練習をしましょう。

1. Life in the city is convenient because there are many shopping centers in the city.
2. We can easily attend our favorite musicians' concerts if we live in the city.
3. We can travel to other cities quite easily by trains and buses.
4. We can see and feel nature when living in the countryside.
5. We can eat fresh and delicious food in the countryside.
6. We can live a quiet life because there are not many cars and trains in the countryside.

They said that _____ . But we don't agree because _____ .

[Hints]

a. It is inconvenient to live in the countryside if there is not much transportation.
b. Large train stations in the city are quite crowded, and it is stressful.
c. There are many cars around shopping centers, so we might have trouble driving smoothly around these areas.
d. There are many wild animals in the countryside, and they sometimes invade people's homes and farms.
e. There are too many people around concert halls, and that makes it uncomfortable for us to live there.
f. We can eat delicious food in restaurants in the city.

NOTE
have trouble -ing「〜するのに苦労する」

Simplified Debate C

以下は、「田舎よりも都会に住む方が良い」というテーマでシンプル・ディベートを行った際の、肯定チームと否定チームの立論です。それぞれの理由と具体例が3つずつ挙げられています。ペアになって、肯定／否定チームに分かれ、相手チームが挙げた理由から2つを選び、それらへの反論を作りましょう。

肯定チーム　　DL 47　CD 47

We think that living in the city is good for the following three reasons. First, it is convenient to live in the city. For example, we can easily go to many shopping centers, movie theaters, and theme parks. Second, there are many activities for people to do. For instance, there are sporting events, plays and concerts all the year round. Lastly, we can travel to other cities quite easily. Most big cities have airports and large train stations, so it is easy for us to visit different parts of the country. Therefore, living in the city has many advantages.

否定チーム　　DL 48　CD 48

We think that living in the countryside is good for the following three reasons. First, we can see and feel nature when living in the countryside. For example, we can always see the mountains and be close to rivers and lakes. Next, fresh food is always available to us when we live in the countryside. For instance, the many fields around the houses are often full of fresh fruit and vegetables during all seasons. Finally, we can live a quiet life. There are not many cars, trains, buses or airports when we live in the countryside. Therefore, living in the countryside has many advantages.

DL 49, 50　CD 49　CD 50

We would like to say two things about their opinions. First, they said that _____ . But we don't agree because _____ _____ . Second, they said that _____ _____ . However, we also disagree with this idea because _____ _____ . Therefore, we don't agree with their opinions.

Unit 15

Simplified Debate 5

聴衆の立場で評価する

Introduction

　シンプル・ディベートを行う時は、ディベーター (debater) として演台の前に立ってスピーチをします。しかし、シンプル・ディベートに参加するのはディベーターだけではありません。進行する司会者 (chairperson) と各スピーチの時間を管理するタイム・キーパー (time keeper) が必要です。そして、ディベートというゲームの勝敗を決めるのは、ディベーターではなく、スピーチを聴いている第三者、すなわち、聴衆 (audience) になります。

　聴衆は、フローシートというディベートで使用するメモ紙でそれぞれのスピーチの要点を聴き取ります。すべてのスピーチの終了後、評価シートを用いて勝敗を決め、記入後に投票箱へ提出します。評価シートでは、「聴き手にスピーチを伝わりやすくする表現が使えているか」、「それぞれの主張に対してきちんと根拠を述べることができているか」などについてチェックをつけるようになっており、その数が多い方がシンプル・ディベートでは勝利となります。

　他者のスピーチを正しく評価することができると、自分がスピーチを作る際や、実際にスピーチを行う際に気をつけなければならないことに気づくことができます。

　本章では、これまで学んだシンプル・ディベートのスピーチの方法・表現の復習と、聴き取りながらメモをとる練習、そして、スピーチの良し悪しを公平・公正に判断し、スコアシートに得点を記入する練習を行います。

Simplified Debate A

ペアになって、「ファストフードを食べるのは良いことである」というテーマでシンプル・ディベートを行います。

Exercise 1

DL 51　CD 51

以下は、肯定チームの立論です。一方の人は立論のスピーチを1分以内で行い、もう一方の人は後に続く評価項目をチェックし、ペアで話し合いましょう。

　We think that eating fast food is good for the following two reasons. First, we can save time by eating fast food when we are busy. For example, fast food restaurants can quickly serve us our food after we order it. Second, fast food is not so expensive. For instance, we can eat *gyudon* for about 400 yen at a *gyudon* shop. Therefore, eating fast food has many advantages.

> - □ 自分の立場をスピーチの最初と最後に述べている。
> - □ 順序を表す表現や具体例を示す表現などを用いてわかりやすく説明している。
> - □ 自分の立場をサポートする適切な理由・具体例など提示している。
> - □ 聴き取りやすいスピードで時間内にスピーチを行っている。
> - □ 意味のまとまりがわかるように発音している。

Exercise 2

DL 52　CD 52

以下は、Exercise 1の立論に対する否定チームの反論です。一方の人は立論のスピーチを1分以内で行い、もう一方の人は後に続く評価項目をチェックし、ペアで話し合いましょう。

　We think that eating fast food is bad for the following two reasons. First, we might gain weight if we eat too much fast food. For example, we can consume more than 300 kilocalories per cheeseburger. Second, we eat fewer vegetables if we eat at fast food restaurants. For instance, we eat only a few slices of onions at *gyudon* restaurants. Therefore, eating fast food has many disadvantages.

> - □ 自分の立場をスピーチの最初と最後に述べている。
> - □ 順序を表す表現や具体例を示す表現などを用いてわかりやすく説明している。
> - □ 自分の立場をサポートする適切な理由・具体例など提示している。
> - □ 聴き取りやすいスピードで時間内にスピーチを行っている。
> - □ 意味のまとまりがわかるように発音している。

Simplified Debate B

Exercise 1

以下のチャートは、「インターネットを使うのは良いことである」というテーマでシンプル・ディベートを行った際の、立論のスピーチの流れを表したものです。後に続く「評価シート」のすべての項目に〇がつくよう、次ページの問題に答えましょう。

> **Chairperson:** Now, we'd like to start the debate. Today's topic is "Using the Internet is good." If necessary, please make notes about this game on your flow chart. DL 53 CD 53

肯定チーム　立論（1分）　　　　　　　　　　　　　　DL 54　CD 54

> **Chairperson:** First of all, we will introduce the affirmative constructive speech within one minute. ［タイム・キーパーはタイマーで1分とセットする］
>
> **Debater A:** We think that using the Internet is good for the following two reasons. ᴬ·＿＿＿＿, we can quickly get a lot of information on the Internet. ᴮ·＿＿＿＿ ᶜ·＿＿＿＿, we can quickly get the latest news by using our own computer and mobile phone. ᴰ·＿＿＿＿, there are many fun websites on the Internet. For instance, we can enjoy listening to music and watching movies for free. ˣ·＿＿＿＿＿＿＿＿＿＿＿＿＿＿＿＿＿＿＿＿＿＿＿＿＿．

否定チーム　立論（1分）　　　　　　　　　　　　　　DL 55　CD 55

> **Chairperson:** Next, we will introduce the negative constructive speech. ［タイム・キーパーはタイマーで1分とセットする］
>
> **Debater B:** We think that using the Internet is bad for the following two reasons. First, there is a lot of incorrect information on the Internet. ʸ·＿＿＿＿＿＿＿＿＿＿＿＿＿＿＿＿＿. Second, using the Internet can cause us some trouble. ᶻ·＿＿＿＿＿＿＿＿＿＿＿＿＿＿＿＿＿＿＿＿＿＿＿＿＿＿＿＿＿＿．Therefore, using the Internet has many disadvantages.

否定チーム　反論（1分）

⬇

肯定チーム　反論（1分）

立論の評価シート

立論	肯定チーム Debater A	否定チーム Debater B
自分の立場をスピーチの最初と最後に述べている。		◯
順序を表す表現や具体例を示す表現などを用いてわかりやすく説明している。		
自分の立場をサポートする適切な理由・具体例など提示している。	◯	
聴き取りやすいスピードで時間内にスピーチを行っている。	◯	◯
意味のまとまりがわかるように発音している。	◯	◯

1. 肯定チームの立論のスピーチの下線部 A〜D に、ふさわしい単語を書き入れましょう。
2. 以下の語句を、肯定チームの立論のスピーチの下線部 X に当てはまるよう正しく並べ替え、書き入れましょう。なお、文頭に来る単語も小文字で表しています。

   [advantages / has / many / the Internet / therefore, / using]

3. [**Hints**] の内容を参考にして、否定チームの立論のスピーチの下線部 Y と Z にふさわしい文を書き入れましょう。

[**Hints**]
- Someone doesn't use the Internet with proper manners. They sometimes post inappropriate content on YouTube.
- Young people tend to get too absorbed in using the Internet, and they might stay awake late at night to play online games.
- People can find out our personal information and misuse it.
- We can see unreliable news on the Internet.

NOTES
with proper manners「正しい方法で」　post ~「~を投稿する」　inappropriate「不適切な」
get too absorbed in ~「~に夢中になりすぎる」　online games「オンラインゲーム」
personal information「個人情報」　misuse ~「~を悪用する」　unreliable「信頼できない」

Unit 15　Simplified Debate 5

Exercise 2

以下のチャートは、「インターネットを使うのは良いことである」というテーマでシンプル・ディベートを行った際の、**Exercise 1**の立論に続く反論のスピーチの流れを表したものです。後に続く「評価シート」のすべての項目に〇がつくよう、次ページの問題に答えましょう。

肯定チーム　立論（1分）

否定チーム　立論（1分）

否定チーム　反論（1分）　　　　　　　　　　　　　　　DL 56　CD 56

Chairperson: Next, we will introduce the negative rebuttal speech.
　　　　　　　　　　　［タイム・キーパーはタイマーで1分とセットする］

Debater C: X._____. First, they said that we can quickly get a lot of information. Y._____ there is also a lot of incorrect information, and it is difficult to judge which information is correct. Second, they said that there are many fun websites on the Internet. However, we also Z._____
_____.
Therefore, we don't agree with their opinions.

肯定チーム　反論（1分）　　　　　　　　　　　　　　　DL 57　CD 57

Chairperson: Next, we will introduce the affirmative rebuttal speech.
　　　　　　　　　　　［タイム・キーパーはタイマーで1分とセットする］

Debater D: X._____. First, they said that there is also a lot of incorrect information on the Internet. Y._____ we can get correct information if we check where the information comes from. Second, they said that people can find out our personal information and misuse it. However, we also disagree with this idea because we can be more careful and reduce the amount of personal information we put on the Internet. Therefore, we don't agree with their opinions.

Chairperson: This finishes the debate. Thank you for your cooperation. Please fill in your score sheet and put it in the ballot box.

反論の評価シート

反論	肯定チーム Debater D	否定チーム Debater C
自分の立場をスピーチの最初と最後に述べている。		
反論をする際の表現を用いながらわかりやすく説明している。		
相手の議論に対しての反論の根拠が明確である。	◯	
聴き取りやすいスピードで時間内にスピーチを行っている。	◯	◯
意味のまとまりがわかるように発音している。	◯	◯

1. 両チームの反論のスピーチの下線部Xにふさわしい一文を書き入れましょう。
2. 両チームの反論のスピーチの下線部Yにふさわしい表現を、5語で書き入れましょう。
3. 以下の語句を、否定チームの反論のスピーチの下線部Zに当てはまるよう正しく並べ替え、書き入れましょう。

   [because / disagree with / harmful software / in these websites / there can be / this idea]

4. 相手チームの立論に対して、どのような反論をしたか、**Exercise 1**の立論も参考にしながら、以下の「フローシート」に日本語でまとめましょう。

■フローシート

		立論	反論
肯定チーム	理由①		理由①への否定側からの反論
	理由②		理由②への否定側からの反論
否定チーム	理由①		理由①への肯定側からの反論
	理由②		理由②への肯定側からの反論

基本文法

5文型

5文型の要素

主語〈S〉 動詞〈V〉 補語〈C〉 目的語〈O〉

5文型の要素にならないもの（文型の確認には不要なもの）

・副詞＝動詞を修飾する、名詞を修飾しない＊

　　　「いつ」「どこで」「どのように」を表す表現（明日、ここで、素早くなども含む）

　＊名詞を修飾するのは形容詞。

・前置詞＊（on, at, in, for, with, by, during など）＋名詞のセット

　＊名詞の「前」に「置く」のが前置詞。

第1文型〈SV〉

主語と動詞だけで文が成立する

She goes *to a swimming pool near her house five times a week*.

I disagree *with you*.

At university she studies *hard*.

I got *to the station at eight o'clock yesterday*.

第2文型〈SVC〉

主語と動詞の後ろの語句がイコールの関係になる（S＝C）

Keiko is a sophomore.

That sounds nice.

I am your instructor.

They become too busy with their part-time job.

Omi beef tastes delicious.

第3文型〈SVO〉

主語と動詞の後ろの語句がイコールの関係ではない（S≠O）

動詞の後ろの語句が動詞の目的語になる

I bought a picture book of dolphins.

Shiga has some high mountains around Lake Biwa.

I enjoy snowboarding with my friends.

Tom got two tickets for the baseball game.

第4文型〈SVOO〉

動詞の後ろに<u>まとまりのある語句が2つある</u>（OO）

動詞の後ろのまとまりのある2つの語句が<u>イコールの関係ではない</u>（O ≠ O）

動詞の後ろのまとまりのある2つの語句が<u>動詞の目的語</u>になる

You usually tell them your name.

This experience will give you a good chance.

I tell you two things.

I will get you some gifts.

第5文型〈SVOC〉（本書では扱っていません）

動詞の後ろに<u>まとまりのある語句が2つある</u>（OC）

動詞の後ろの2つの語句が<u>イコールの関係になる</u>（O = C）

She named her dog *Kuro*.

The news made me happy.

They painted the room green.

be 動詞と一般動詞

動詞〈V〉には、be 動詞と一般動詞があり、これらの動詞の「形」を変えることで現在・過去・未来の時間（時制）を示します。

現在：動詞の現在形

過去：動詞の過去形

未来：動詞の前に will や be going to を付ける（「未来形」はない）

be 動詞

現在形 am / are / is

過去形 was / were

一般動詞（be 動詞以外の動詞）

現在形：主語が三人称単数*の時は語尾に s/es が付く

過去形：規則変化では語尾に ed が付く、不規則変化にも注意

一般動詞と be 動詞の未来

will ＋動詞の原形

am / are / is ＋ going to ＋動詞の原形

＊三人称単数とは？

「私」でも、目の前にいる「あなた（たち）」でもない第三者（he、student**s**、desk、book**s**）で、1つ（1人）しか存在しない＝2つ（2人）以上の存在ではないもの（he、~~student**s**~~、desk、~~book**s**~~）

基本文法

be 動詞と一般動詞では、否定文や疑問文の作り方が異なります。また、Unit 3 で学ぶ「頻度の副詞」の入る位置も違います。

be 動詞

- 疑問文：主語と be 動詞の前後を入れ替えて、最後に？を付ける
  Is Keiko a sophomore**?**
- 否定文：be 動詞の後ろに not を付ける
  Keiko **isn't (is not)** a sophomore.
- 頻度の副詞：be 動詞の<u>後ろ</u>に置く
  Keiko is **never** late for classes.

一般動詞（be 動詞以外の動詞）

- 疑問文：Do / Does / Did ＋主語＋動詞の原形に、最後に？を付ける
  Do you agree with me**?**
- 否定文：do not (don't) / does not (doesn't) / did not (didn't) ＋動詞の原形
  I **don't (do not)** agree with you.
- 頻度の副詞：一般動詞の前に置く
  He **always** disagrees with me.

例文とそのポイント

Marie enjoy**s** shopping with her friends.
→主語が三人称単数なので、一般動詞の語尾に s が付く

Does Marie **enjoy** shopping with her friends?
Marie **does**n't **enjoy** shopping with her friends.
→ does で現在を表しているので、一般動詞の enjoy は原形

Marie **did**n't **enjoy** shopping with her friends.
→ did で過去を表しているので、一般動詞の enjoy は原形

I **usually** practice judo.
→一般動詞なので、頻度の副詞は一般動詞の前に

You are **always** busy these days.
→ be 動詞なので、頻度の副詞は be 動詞の後に

本書には CD（別売）があります

Speak Easy

From Basic Conversation to Simplified Debate

会話からディベートまで スピーキング基本演習

2019 年 1 月 20 日　初版第 1 刷発行
2025 年 2 月 20 日　初版第 10 刷発行

著　者　　藤　岡　克　則
　　　　　山　内　信　幸
　　　　　Neil Heffernan
　　　　　金　﨑　茂　樹
　　　　　橋　尾　晋　平
発行者　　福　岡　正　人
発行所　　株式会社　**金　星　堂**

（〒 101-0051）東京都千代田区神田神保町 3-21
Tel.（03）3263-3828（営業部）
Tel.（03）3263-3997（編集部）
Fax（03）3263-0716
https://www.kinsei-do.co.jp

編集担当　松本明子　　　　　　　　　Printed in Japan
印刷所・製本所／倉敷印刷株式会社
本書の無断複製・複写は著作権法上での例外を除き禁じられています。
本書を代行業者等の第三者に依頼してスキャンやデジタル化すること
は、たとえ個人や家庭内での利用であっても認められておりません。
落丁・乱丁本はお取り替えいたします。

ISBN978-4-7647-4084-6 C1082